Congressional Research Service

Pilotless Drones: Background and Considerations for Congress Regarding Unmanned Aircraft Operations in the National Airspace System

Bart Elias
Specialist in Aviation Policy

September 10, 2012

Congressional Research Service

7-5700

www.crs.gov

R42718

CRS Report for Congress ———————————

Prepared for Members and Committees of Congress

Summary

Growing interest in the use of unmanned aerial vehicles (UAVs), particularly for homeland security and law enforcement applications, has spurred considerable debate over how to accommodate these unmanned aircraft and keep them safely separated from other air traffic. Additionally, the use of these pilotless aircraft, popularly referred to as drones, for aerial surveillance and law enforcement purposes has raised specific concerns regarding privacy and Fourth Amendment rights and potential intrusiveness. These issues have come to the forefront in policy debate in response to provisions in the FAA Modernization and Reform Act of 2012 (P.L. 112-95) that require the Federal Aviation Administration (FAA) to begin integrating unmanned aircraft into the national airspace system by the end of FY2015.

While drones have been used extensively by the military and small radio-controlled model aircraft have been around for more than 50 years, advances in more complex vehicle controls and imaging sensor capabilities are spurring public sector and commercial interest in unmanned aircraft for a variety of purposes, including law enforcement, homeland security, aerial imaging, and scientific research. FAA currently approves public entities (such as federal agencies, public universities, and local police departments) to operate UAVs on a case-by-case basis, but growing interest is making this approach increasingly untenable. Moreover, commercial users are seeking authorization to fly drones, but so far FAA has only allowed test and demonstration flights by manufacturers. FAA faces a number of challenges to address anticipated growth in demand for civilian UAV operations and develop regulations governing the certification and operation of unmanned aircraft systems in domestic airspace.

Congress has generally supported efforts to integrate unmanned aircraft into the national airspace system and foster growth in the unmanned aircraft industry. It enacted extensive provisions in P.L. 112-95 that are designed to streamline and accelerate the operation of unmanned aircraft in domestic airspace by both public entities and commercial operators. Notably, that law requires FAA to issue regulations pertaining to the operation of small UAVs (weighing less than 55 pounds) and requires FAA to create and implement a plan to begin the integration of unmanned aircraft into the national airspace system by the end of FY2015. Toward that goal, the act requires FAA to establish six test ranges throughout the United States to study unmanned aircraft integration technical issues.

The act establishes an ambitious timeline for FAA to grapple with and resolve a number of complex issues regarding the safety and security of unmanned aircraft operations. Furthermore, aircraft operators have expressed specific concerns that drone operations should not result in airspace restrictions or other measures that could limit accessibility to the national airspace system.

In addition to these various challenges, the privacy implications and potential intrusiveness of drone operations have emerged as a significant issue before Congress. Civil liberties and privacy groups have cautioned that voluntary industry measures, including a code of conduct to, among other things, respect privacy, are inadequate to assure that drones will not be misused in ways that could infringe upon the privacy of individuals and intrude upon their daily activities. Moreover, FAA's authority over specific uses of civilian unmanned aircraft appears limited so long as safety and national security are not compromised, raising additional concerns that future drone operations could lead to complaints and lawsuits over noise, intrusiveness, and interference with the use and enjoyment of public or private property.

Contents

Background

In the early 2000s, military and intelligence use of unmanned aircraft systems (UASs)[1] in Afghanistan and Iraq spurred interest in potential domestic use of these systems. The safe integration of unmanned aircraft in the crowded airspace above the United States poses a number of regulatory challenges for the Federal Aviation Administration (FAA) and raises some unique legal and ethical questions. These issues have come to the forefront following enactment of the FAA Modernization and Reform Act of 2012 (P.L. 112-95), which requires FAA to begin integrating unmanned aircraft into the national airspace system by the end of FY2015.

Military Roots

While much of the policy debate surrounding civilian use of unmanned aircraft is new, unmanned aircraft have been used by the military since the early days of aviation. During World War I, the Navy funded research to develop a prototype flying bomb called the Hewitt-Sperry Automatic Airplane. Building on this concept, the first full-scale powered unmanned aerial vehicles, the Curtiss-Sperry Flying Bomb and the Kettering Aerial Torpedo, nicknamed the "Bug," were developed in 1918 as unpiloted bomb delivery platforms. The "Bug" was designed to fly a pre-set course, then shed its wings delivering an explosive payload that would detonate on impact. It was never used in combat, and further development was halted in the 1920s.[2] As evidenced by these early prototypes, the U.S. military has long had an interest in unmanned aircraft, which evolved into the development of several successful guided missile designs during World War II.

The military has used autonomous target drones and remotely piloted vehicles extensively since the 1950s. These vehicles first served as targets for training combat pilots and as decoys in combat arenas, but their roles evolved with advances in sensor technology, allowing them to take on more advanced aerial reconnaissance roles.

In the 1980s, spurred by Israeli initiatives, the military developed more sophisticated unmanned systems with extensive ground-based command and control capabilities. Unmanned aircraft were used by U.S. forces for intelligence missions in the Balkans in the late 1990s, and in Afghanistan and Iraq for reconnaissance and surveillance as well as, more recently, for combat missions.[3] In support of military research, development, testing, and training, the military now operates unmanned aircraft extensively in U.S. airspace. The military services work closely with FAA to designate special use airspace for conducting unmanned aircraft operations, typically over military bases or sparsely populated land.

---

[1] Unmanned aircraft systems (UASs) refer to aircraft that fly without onboard pilots along with ground control stations, networks, and personnel needed to operate these aircraft. Unmanned aerial vehicles (UAVs) refer to the unmanned aircraft in these systems, which are often referred to as drones in the media. The terms UAVs, unmanned aircraft, and drones are used interchangeably throughout this report.

[2] Kettering Aerial Torpedo Bug, *Fact Sheet*, National Museum of the Air Force: Dayton, Ohio, available at http://www.nationalmuseum.af mil/factsheets/factsheet.asp?id=320.

[3] For further information on military and intelligence UASs see CRS Report R42136, *U.S. Unmanned Aerial Systems*, by Jeremiah Gertler.

From Longtime Hobby to a Burgeoning Civilian Market

Until recently, civilian interest in operating unmanned aircraft in U.S. airspace had largely been limited to long-standing hobbyist use of radio-controlled model aircraft. The Academy of Model Aeronautics, a national organization representing model aviation enthusiasts, was founded in 1936 and claims a membership of more than 150,000.[4] It serves as the chartering organization for more than 2,400 model airplane clubs across the United States. At present, radio-controlled model aircraft operate under a voluntary standard that generally permits flights only below 400 feet above the surface. These guidelines specify that model aircraft be flown away from populated areas and not in close proximity to full-scale aircraft. They further request coordination with air traffic facilities when planning operations within 3 miles of an airport and suggest that model aircraft be adequately flight tested before being operated in front of spectators.[5]

While most radio-controlled model aircraft are powered by small propeller engines and weigh only a few pounds, some are jet-powered scale models weighing over 100 pounds. The distinction between functional model aircraft and small unmanned aerial vehicles is, therefore, largely based on an aircraft's use rather than its size or capabilities: whereas model aircraft are regarded as being used for recreational purposes, UAVs serve public use missions, such as law enforcement and disaster relief, and commercial applications. The prospect of robust growth in use of UAVs had triggered more formal analysis of the process for granting approvals and development of regulations for UAV operations. The challenges associated with safely integrating civilian UAVs into domestic airspace are discussed in detail below (see "Domestic Airspace Integration Issues").

Flight missions considered to be "dirty, dull, or dangerous" are regarded as prime candidates for the use of unmanned aircraft. Examples include aerial surveillance missions for homeland security, border protection, and law enforcement; highway traffic monitoring; forest fire scouting; disaster response; aerial applications of pesticides; pipeline and transmission line inspection; aerial surveying and geospatial imaging; atmospheric and environmental science; wildlife and natural resources management; scientific data collection; and hurricane and severe storm monitoring. Some industry experts foresee eventual use of unmanned aircraft for cargo transport. At this point, however, passenger-carrying UAVs are not on the horizon.

Industry analysts anticipate a robust market for unmanned aircraft systems, although the extent to which civilian sales will contribute to this market is highly dependent on how the regulation of civilian drones proceeds. The Teal Group, an aviation and aerospace consulting firm, predicted that, over the next ten years, annual spending on unmanned aircraft systems and sensor payloads will increase by 73% and worldwide spending on unmanned aircraft systems will total $89 billion, with the United States accounting for 62% of the research and development spending and 55% of procurement totals.[6] Similarly, VisionGain, a UK-based business information provider, foresees strong demand for unmanned aircraft payloads and subsystems, as well for UAV flight training and simulation.[7]

---

[4] For additional information see the Academy of Model Aeronautics (AMA) website at http://www.modelaircraft.org.

[5] Federal Aviation Administration, *Model Aircraft Operating Standards*, Advisory Circular AC 91-57, June 9, 1981, Washington, DC.

[6] Teal Group Corporation, *Teal Group Predicts Worldwide UAV Market Will Total $89 Billion in Its 2012 UAV Market Profile and Forecast*, available at http://tealgroup.com/index.php/about-teal/teal-group-in-the-media/3/79-teal-group-predicts-worldwide-uav-market-will-total-89-billion-in-its-2012-uav-market-profile-and-forecast.

[7] VisionGain, *The UAV Payload and Subsystem Market 2012-2022*, July 19, 2012, available at (continued...)

Unmanned Aircraft Designs

Unmanned aircraft come in all shapes and sizes. They range in size from bug-sized "nano drones" to vehicles the size and weight of large business jets. Small UAVs have an upper weight limit of 55 pounds. Typical civilian drones are likely to fall in the range of a few pounds up to that weight limit, while medium-sized unmanned aircraft, like the MQ-9 Predator 2/Reaper (with a 65-foot wingspan and a maximum takeoff weight of about 10,000 pounds) may be used on more specialized, medium-altitude and high-altitude, long-duration missions like border and maritime patrols and environmental research missions. Unmanned aircraft include fixed-wing airplanes, helicopters, rotorcraft, and even blimps. Unmanned aircraft may also include certain vehicles, referred to as optionally piloted vehicles, that are capable of being flown by a pilot as a conventional aircraft or being operated remotely or autonomously depending on mission conditions, needs, and requirements. **Figure 1** provides a montage of various unmanned systems illustrating a range of different vehicle sizes and designs including (clockwise from top left) the hand-launched AeroVironment RQ-20 Puma; an unmanned version of the Kaman K-MAX external load helicopter operated by the U.S. Marine Corps; the Honeywell RQ-16 "Tarantula" T-Hawk; the AAI RQ-2 Pioneer; and the "Altair" variant of the General Atomics MQ-9 Predator 2/Reaper.

Figure 1. A Variety of Small to Medium-Sized Unmanned Aircraft Designs

Sources: Clockwise from top left, U.S. Army, U.S. Marine Corps, U.S. Army, U.S. Army, National Oceanographic and Atmospheric Administration (NOAA).

(...continued)

http://www.visiongain.com/Report/857/The-UAV-Payload-and-Subsystems-Market-2012-2022; VisionGain, *The UAV Flight Training & Simulation Market 2012-2022*, May 17, 2012, available at http://www.visiongain.com/Report/823/The-UAV-Flight-Training-Simulation-Market-2012-2022.

While a substantial portion of this market will be accounted for by the defense sector, manufacturers are increasingly looking toward the civilian sector, fearing that military sales may stagnate as operations in Afghanistan are scaled back and U.S. defense budgets grow tighter. However, some forecasters have concluded that growth in the civilian market is unlikely until a regulatory framework allowing routine UAS operations is established.[8] FAA anticipates that once such regulations are put in place, roughly 10,000 active civilian UASs will commence operations within the first five years.[9]

It is important to distinguish public-use missions from purely civilian activities involving UAVs, although certain commercial operations, such as utility line inspection, may serve a public benefit. The distinction matters because aircraft owned or leased by federal and state agencies, counties, and municipalities, are regulated differently from civil aircraft operated by private individuals and corporations.[10] Although the regulatory distinctions are complex, in general, FAA oversight and authority over public-use aircraft are more limited. For this reason, some public-sector entities, particularly homeland security and law enforcement agencies and public universities, are already making limited use of UAVs while the commercial market awaits FAA regulatory action.

Congressional Interest and Related Legislation

Congress has generally been supportive of efforts to integrate unmanned aircraft into the national airspace system and foster growth in the unmanned aircraft industry. Through oversight and legislation, it has pushed FAA to accelerate its regulatory processes regarding the certification and operation of unmanned aircraft.

UAVs in Vision 100—The Century of Aviation Reauthorization Act

In 2003, Congress included language in Vision 100—The Century of Aviation Reauthorization Act (P.L. 108-176) specifying that the Next Generation Air Transportation System (NextGen), which FAA is developing to handle air traffic control, shall "accommodate a wide range of aircraft operations, including airlines, air taxis, helicopters, general aviation, and *unmanned aerial vehicles*."[11] That language set the stage for ongoing policy and technical consideration of how to best accommodate unmanned aircraft in the future airspace system.

While unmanned aircraft were only briefly mentioned in the act, the specific language requiring that they be accommodated in the design of NextGen served as an important step toward recognizing that drones would likely play a significant role in the aviation system of the future. Nearly a decade later, unmanned aircraft have evolved considerably, and the importance of

---

[8] U.S. Government Accountability Office, *Unmanned Aircraft Systems: Use in the National Airspace System and the Role of the Department of Homeland Security*, Statement of Gerald L. Dillingham, Ph.D., Director, Physical Infrastructure Issues, Before the Subcommittee on Oversight, Investigations, and Management, Committee on Homeland Security, House of Representatives, July 19, 2012, GAO-12-889T.

[9] Federal Aviation Administration, *FAA Aerospace Forecasts FY2012-2032*, p. 57.

[10] 49 U.S.C. §40125 specifies the qualifications for public aircraft status.

[11] P.L. 107-76, Section 709c(6), italics added.

considering them in aviation regulation and the design and operation of the national airspace system has become a major policy and technical consideration.

Provisions of the FAA Modernization and Reform Act of 2012

During debate over the most recent FAA reauthorization, the integration of unmanned aircraft in national airspace was an issue of considerable interest. The resulting legislation, the FAA Modernization and Reform Act of 2012 (P.L. 112-95) contained extensive provisions designed to promote and facilitate the use of civilian unmanned aircraft. These included mandates for

- development of an integration plan that is to commence by the end of FY2015, if not sooner, along with a five-year roadmap for achieving integration objectives;

- selection of six test sites to study UAV integration into the national airspace system;

- designation of certain permanent areas in the Arctic where small unmanned aircraft may operate 24 hours per day for commercial and research purposes, including flights conducted beyond line-of-sight;

- a simplified process for issuing authorizations for entities seeking to operate public UASs in the national airspace system;

- a collaborative process to incrementally expand airspace access as technology matures and safety data and analysis become available, and to facilitate public agency access to UAS test ranges;

- a requirement to develop and implement operational and certification requirements for public UASs by December 31, 2015; and

- an exemption from rules and regulations pertaining to the operation of unmanned aircraft for model aircraft weighing 55 pounds or less that are flown within visual line-of-sight strictly for hobby or recreation.

Current FAA Policy and Oversight

The provisions in P.L. 112-95 reflect a general view that FAA's slow progress to date on addressing regulatory requirements for unmanned aircraft may be a barrier to civilian drone operations. While FAA has been studying unmanned aircraft operations for almost a decade, it continues to address requests to operate unmanned aircraft on a case-by-case basis. This approach is becoming increasingly untenable as growing numbers of public and commercial entities seek authorization to operate unmanned aircraft in domestic airspace.

On February 13, 2007, FAA issued a notice of policy declaring that "no person may operate a UAS in the National Airspace System without specific authority."[12] This policy applies to both public and private unmanned aircraft. FAA currently has two methods for granting authority to operate unmanned aircraft, depending on whether the operator is a public or a private entity.

[12] Federal Aviation Administration, "Unmanned Aircraft Operations in the National Airspace System," *Federal Register*, 72(39), February 13, 2007, 6689-6690.

Current Approvals Process

Unmanned aircraft operated by the military or other federal, state, or local agencies must obtain a Certificate of Waiver or Authorization (COA) from FAA. Since 2006, FAA has issued COAs to more than 100 unique public entities throughout the United States, ranging from local fire departments to research laboratories. Since the COAs have narrow scopes and durations, entities must obtain new authorizations every few months. In 2009, FAA issued 146 such COAs. In 2010, the number of COAs issued grew to 298.[13] Although FAA has streamlined its approval process, as required by P.L. 112-95, growing interest in operating unmanned aircraft from public entities is expected to place strains on the current case-by-case approach to authorization.

Additionally, in much the same manner as manned aircraft developers and builders must obtain FAA certification to test fly their aircraft, a number of drone developers have received special airworthiness certificates in the experimental category. Special airworthiness certificates, which offer the only legal route for private entities to operate unmanned aircraft for commercial purposes, have been issued on a limited basis for flight tests, demonstrations, and training.

FAA has raised concerns that other civilian users are operating commercial UAVs under the voluntary guidelines issued in the early 1980s that were intended to apply only to recreational users of model aircraft. As previously described, these guidelines advise such users to maintain altitudes lower than 400 feet above the ground, select sites away from populated and noise-sensitive areas, give right of way to full-scale aircraft, and advise airport operators and air traffic facilities if operating within 3 miles of an airport. The FAA statement of policy clarifies that these general guidelines alone are not sufficient for commercial operators of unmanned aircraft, regardless of the size of such aircraft. The FAA did, however, indicate that it has undertaken a safety review to determine whether certain small, slow-moving unmanned aircraft could be safely operated under a similar set of guidelines without requiring special airworthiness certification.

Regulating Small Unmanned Aircraft

Developers of small-scale unmanned aircraft are concerned that FAA has been moving too slowly on measures to safely accommodate these types of aircraft. Since 2007, industry has been pushing for separate regulations for "ultralight, low-speed, short-life UASs that will not be flying over populated areas or in controlled airspace," arguing that a one-size-fits-all approach to regulation would not likely be effective given the wide range of systems being considered for civilian use.[14]

Other than streamlining the case-by-case approvals process, FAA has not taken any formal action addressing the regulation of civilian small unmanned aircraft. After several delays, FAA plans to release a proposed rule regarding the certification and operation of small unmanned aircraft systems (sUAS) in October 2012, as a step toward meeting the August 2014 statutory deadline for issuance of a final rule. Additionally, P.L. 112-95 directed FAA to assess whether certain unmanned aircraft operations do not pose a safety hazard or a threat to national security and can therefore safely be allowed. Actions to address this mandate are currently in progress.

---

[13] Federal Aviation Administration, *Fact Sheet: Unmanned Aircraft Systems (UAS)*, Updated July 2011, available at http://www.faa.gov/about/initiatives/uas/media/UAS_FACT_Sheet.pdf.

[14] David Hughes, "Civil Use of Unmanned Aircraft Systems Could Grow Rapidly," *Aviation Week and Space Technology*, February 12, 2007, p. 49.

Wide Scale Integration of Unmanned Aircraft in Domestic Airspace

UAV manufacturers and users are seeking a regulatory structure for the certification of UAV systems and approval for operation in domestic airspace. Ideally, operators of approved systems want the ability to "file and fly," meaning that they would be granted vehicle certification with broad operating authority akin to current manned aircraft certification standards. Such regulation would potentially allow unmanned aircraft operators to file routine flight plans, or in some cases simply carry out flight operations without any specific notification requirements, much as manned aircraft do.[15] While FAA's approach to address the mandates set forth in P.L. 112-95 regarding unmanned aircraft integration into the national airspace system is yet to be defined, it is most likely that FAA regulation and oversight of UAVs will adopt an evolving, risk-based approach toward this end goal of seamless integration.

As a first step, P.L. 112-95 mandated that FAA identify six test sites to specifically test concepts and technologies for integrated unmanned aircraft operations. FAA held public meetings and webinars and solicited public comments on the selection of test sites in March 2012, but has not yet gone through a formal source selection process or announced further details regarding test site selection, even though it was mandated to identify the sites by the summer of 2012 and have at least one site operational by February 2013.

Under P.L. 112-95, FAA is also required to develop a comprehensive plan to safely accelerate integration of civilian unmanned aircraft into the national airspace system as soon as practical but not later than September 2015. Meeting this mandate will require extensive research and regulatory action over the next three years.

Domestic Airspace Integration Issues

Key challenges to drone integration in domestic airspace include safety concerns, potential security risks, and concerns regarding airspace restrictions and possible disruptions to manned flight operations.

Safety Concerns

Threshold criteria for integrated unmanned aircraft operations are that UAVs do not pose undue risk other aircraft or compromise safety to persons or property on the ground.[16] To meet safety objectives, UASs will require technology and standard procedures for sensing and avoiding other air traffic under all possible scenarios, including lost communications. System reliability and human factors are important systems design considerations, as are training and qualification standards for drone pilots, unmanned aircraft systems operators, and other safety-critical personnel.[17]

---

[15] Katherine McIntire Peters and Beth Dickey, "Droning On," Government Executive, October 15, 2004, pp. 68-76.

[16] Federal Aviation Administration, *Fact Sheet: Unmanned Aircraft Systems (UAS)*, Updated July 2011, available at http://www.faa.gov/about/initiatives/uas/media/UAS_FACT_Sheet.pdf.

[17] *Drone pilots* refers to ground personnel responsible for direct flight control of the unmanned vehicle whereas the term *systems operators* refers to personnel responsible for operating sensor payloads or other aircraft systems, such as fuel systems, that do not involve direct manipulation of flight controls or flight guidance systems. Other safety critical (continued...)

Sensing and Avoiding Other Air Traffic

Domestic airspace accommodates more than 70,000 flights per day[18] at a variety of altitudes, including low- and high-altitude military training flights, high-altitude air carrier and business jet flights, medium-altitude commuter and general aviation flights, and low-altitude recreational and sightseeing flights and helicopter operations. The risk of collision between these users and unmanned aircraft must be adequately mitigated before unmanned aircraft can routinely utilize the national airspace system.

The Government Accountability Office (GAO) concluded that no suitable technology is currently available to provide unmanned aircraft, particularly small UAVs, with the detect, sense, and avoid requirements needed to safely operate within the national airspace system. GAO noted that small unmanned aircraft pose a particular challenge because they operate at low altitudes. Many other aircraft operating at these altitudes do not use electronic transponders to broadcast their position and altitude, and in any case many small UAVs lack the ability to receive transponder signals. The needed equipment is simply too large and heavy to install on many small UAVs.[19]

Currently, these limitations substantially restrict UAV operations to line-of-sight scenarios, where operators on the ground or spotters in chase planes can provide the necessary capabilities to detect and avoid other air traffic. FAA is currently evaluating options for routinely allowing small unmanned aircraft to use line-of-sight as an acceptable means to detect and avoid manned aircraft under a regulatory regime for small UAVs.

For more sophisticated medium and large-sized UAVs seeking approval for operations beyond line of sight, technology advancements are needed to assure safety in an environment shared with manned flights. Remote sensing capabilities, including onboard cameras, airborne radars, and equipment to interrogate aircraft transponder signals (similar to the traffic collision avoidance systems on jetliners) can combine to provide operators with robust air traffic information.

An emerging technology, Automated Dependent Surveillance-Broadcast (ADS-B) will be required on manned aircraft by 2020 and will serve as the principal means for aircraft tracking under NextGen. Using ADS-B, aircraft will broadcast precise global positioning system (GPS) location information to air traffic controllers and other air traffic, potentially including unmanned aircraft. While ADS-B may provide unmanned aircraft operators with the capability to gather precise position and flight path information for nearby air traffic in the future, backup systems will likely be needed because ADS-B transmission and reception may not be guaranteed all the time.

(...continued)

personnel may include maintenance personnel and equipment technicians that service the air vehicle, the ground station or command and control linkages between the vehicle and the ground station.

[18] Based on 2010 total combined aircraft operations at towered airports reported in Federal Aviation Administration, *FAA Aerospace Forecasts FY2012-2032.* This does not include activity at non-towered airports and, therefore, understates the total number of daily flights, for which there is no definitive count.

[19] U.S. Government Accountability Office, *Unmanned Aircraft Systems: Use in the National Airspace System and the Role of the Department of Homeland Security*, Statement of Gerald L. Dillingham, Ph.D., Director, Physical Infrastructure Issues, Before the Subcommittee on Oversight, Investigations, and Management, Committee on Homeland Security, House of Representatives, July 19, 2012, GAO-12-889T.

FAA has not specifically approved any technology or suite of technologies as being sufficient to provide acceptable "sense and avoid" capabilities.[20] Part of the challenge is that existing technologies do not assure avoidance capabilities under all operational conditions, including autonomous UAV operations or in situations when UAVs lose their command guidance links with ground control facilities. Standardized procedures for responding when UAV guidance has been lost are currently lacking, but will be needed to ensure that air traffic controllers and airspace managers can redirect nearby traffic and mitigate collision risks.

No single technology is likely to address the complex sense and avoid requirements that are critical for unmanned aircraft integration. FAA has been working closely with RTCA, Inc., which functions as a federal advisory committee on aviation technologies, to develop consensus standards regarding minimum aviation system performance standards for sense and avoid technologies as well as for command, control, and communications systems for unmanned aircraft systems.[21] RTCA has been performing this work under its standards committee on unmanned aircraft systems (SC-203), which is scheduled to complete its work on these issues by December 2013 and intends to publish recommended standards soon thereafter. These standards, along with findings from unmanned aircraft integration testing, will likely form the basis of FAA regulations and guidance regarding sense and avoid technologies and UAV operating procedures.

Mitigating Risks to Persons and Property on the Ground

In addition to risks to other air traffic, unmanned aircraft operations may pose a risk to persons and property on the ground. Thus far, unmanned aircraft testing and operational use, such as for military testing and training and for border and maritime patrol operations, have been conducted largely over sparsely populated areas. In the future, however, law enforcement and commercial users are expected to undertake flights over densely populated areas, a prospect which raises specific concerns over safety procedures. For example, to minimize the likelihood of a crash when communications, command, and control linkages between the vehicle and the ground control station are disrupted, UAVs may need the ability to autonomously return to base.

Drone crashes, such as the 2006 crash of an MQ-9 Predator B drone operated by Customs and Border Protection (CBP) near Nogales, NM, and the more recent crash of a Navy RQ-4A Global Hawk near Salisbury, MD in June, 2012, have raised public concern over the safety of unmanned aircraft operations. While drone safety has improved considerably over the past decade, the accident rate for unmanned aircraft is still far above that of manned aircraft, although direct comparisons are difficult, given that most drone operations examined have involved riskier flying during development and testing and in war and conflict zones.[22]

The risk posed to persons and property on the ground is a function of both crash likelihood and the potential consequences in terms of loss of life, injury, or property damage. While smaller

---

[20] "Sense and avoid" refers to technologies and capabilities allowing unmanned aircraft to reliably detect other air traffic and maneuver away from such traffic in a manner that adequately mitigates collision risks.

[21] RTCA was organized in 1935 as the Radio Technical Commission for Aeronautics. Today it operates as a private, not-for-profit corporation. Its recommendations are used by FAA as a basis for policy, program, and regulatory decisions.

[22] Roland E. Weibel and R. John Hansman, *Safety Considerations for Operation of Unmanned Aerial Vehicles in the National Airspace System*, MIT International Center for Air Transportation, Department of Aeronautics and Astronautics, Massachusetts Institute of Technology, Cambridge, MA, March 2005, Report No. ICAT-2005-1.

UAVs may be expected to crash more frequently, the potential for catastrophic consequences is less given that these vehicles do not weigh enough or carry enough fuel to cause major damage on the ground. On the other hand, larger UAVs, like the MQ-9 Reaper or the RQ-4 Global Hawk, can potentially cause as much damage as a mid- to large-sized corporate jet. However, safety considerations in the design and operation of these more complex systems may reduce the likelihood of a crash. Additional procedures that can be incorporated into safety regulations for unmanned aircraft systems may further mitigate flight risks. These procedures may include

- formal risk assessments for systems certification and mission planning;

- development of ground impact models and mitigation plans to reduce risks to persons and property on the ground;[23] and

- structured training and certification requirements for unmanned aircraft pilots, systems operators, and other safety critical personnel.

Human Factors Considerations

The issue of training and certification requirements for unmanned aircraft systems personnel raises a much broader issue regarding the role of humans in these systems. Indeed, the term *unmanned* aircraft system (UAS) is a misnomer: while the aircraft themselves may be unmanned, the systems needed to operate them safely depend extensively on human interaction. Although drones operate without a pilot on board, human performance is a major consideration in setting policy for the integration of unmanned aircraft systems in domestic airspace. Key human factors to be considered include operator interfaces and controls and the training and qualifications of drone pilots, systems operators, and other safety critical personnel.

The previously mentioned 2006 crash of a UAV operated by Customs and Border Protection (CBP) illustrates the importance of these human factors considerations. On April 25, 2006, a Predator B (MQ-9) drone crashed in a remote area along the U.S.-Mexico border near Nogales, AZ following a loss of engine power. The National Transportation Safety Board (NTSB) determined that the probable cause of the mishap was the drone pilot's failure to follow appropriate procedures when switching to an alternate control console in the ground control station following a computer malfunction.[24] The error resulted in the pilot inadvertently cutting off the vehicle's fuel supply.

CBP had only been operating the Predator B aircraft since September 2005, eight months prior to the mishap. NTSB concluded that during this time CBP was providing a minimal amount of operational oversight of its UAS program and cited its inadequate surveillance of the program as a contributing factor in the crash.

The NTSB investigation revealed that, despite repeated computer malfunctions, neither CBP nor its contractors had a program in place to ensure that maintenance tasks were performed correctly or that corrective measures were applied. The NTSB investigation also found that while the mishap pilot had only 27 hours of flight time with the Predator B model, and had only been given

---

[23] Ibid.

[24] National Transportation Safety Board, NTSB Identification: CHI06MA121, Aviation Accident Database & Synopses, Probable Cause Approval Date: October 31, 2007. Available at http://www.ntsb.gov/aviationquery/ brief.aspx?ev_id=20060509X00531&key=1.

verbal approval to fly the vehicle accompanied by an instructor pilot, the instructor pilot was not present in the ground control station when the error occurred. NTSB further noted that the verbal approval was not standard practice for CBP.

The incident illustrates that, despite the lack of an onboard pilot, human performance considerations are critical in the design of unmanned aircraft systems. The failure that led to the crash was preventable had the system been designed and operated with certain safeguards in place to compensate for human fallibility. Greater attention to human factors considerations in the design and operation of unmanned aircraft systems and in the development of training programs and operational procedures could improve safety and facilitate the integration of unmanned aircraft in the national airspace system.

Operator Training and Qualification

One particularly important human factors consideration for regulators is a determination regarding training standards and minimum qualification requirements for personnel involved in flight operations. The appropriate training and qualifications may depend in part on the size of the aircraft and the complexity of the system, as a "one size fits all" approach may be inappropriate given the diversity among vehicles, systems, and operational missions.

Currently the U.S. Air Force requires its Predator/Reaper and Global Hawk pilots to be pilot-rated military officers.[25] The other military services do not require drones to be operated by rated pilots, but do require specialized training. It is uncertain how these different approaches may serve as a basis for FAA to develop training requirements and qualification standards for civilian UAV pilots and operators, as military approaches vary considerably and are tailored to specific systems and missions.

One approach would be for FAA to develop basic training and certification standards for operators of small UAVs, while requiring more elaborate training and certification requirements for personnel seeking to operate or maintain large, complex unmanned aircraft systems. The extent to which requirements for UAV personnel may overlap with requirements for piloting or maintaining manned aircraft remains uncertain but could have significant implications for the industry's development. One perceived advantage of unmanned aircraft over manned aircraft is lower operating costs, and mandating that unmanned systems have highly trained pilots and operators with specialized certifications could reduce that potential cost advantage.

Another issue may involve medical certification. Medical conditions or poor eyesight preclude some individuals from obtaining pilot certification, and the rigors of the flight environment demand stringent medical requirements. Given the significant differences in the work environment and the potential consequences of medical problems in an aircraft compared to inside a ground control station, FAA may choose to relax some medical requirements to allow certain individuals that would otherwise not be medically fit to fly to operate unmanned aircraft.

---

[25] See CRS Report R42136, *U.S. Unmanned Aerial Systems*, by Jeremiah Gertler.

Addressing Potential Security Risks

In addition to safety risks, the operation of civilian unmanned aircraft in domestic airspace raises potential security risks, including the possibility that terrorists could use a drone to carry out an attack against a ground target. It is also possible that drones themselves could be targeted by terrorists or cybercriminals seeking to tap into sensor data transmissions or to cause mayhem by hacking or jamming command and control signals.

Drone Weapons

Terrorists could potentially use drones to carry out small-scale attacks using explosives, or as platforms for chemical, biological, or radiological attacks. In September 2011, the FBI arrested Rezwan Ferdaus, a U.S. citizen from Ashland, MA, charging him in a terrorist plot to attack the Pentagon and the Capitol using large model aircraft packed with high explosives. While the small payload of the model aircraft may have limited the lethality of the explosions, Ferdaus planned to recruit others to use assault rifles to target people fleeing the Pentagon after the drone attack.[26] In July 2012, Ferdaus pleaded guilty to attempting to provide material support to terrorists and attempting to damage and destroy federal buildings by means of an explosive in a plea agreement under which additional charges were dropped. The incident has raised specific concerns about potential terrorist attacks using unmanned aircraft, although the payload capacities of small UAVs would limit the damage these attacks could inflict using only conventional explosives.

Intentional Hacking and Signal Jamming

Additionally, unmanned aircraft command and control links could potentially be intentionally jammed or hacked resulting in a loss or hostile takeover of control. For example, Todd Humphreys, an assistant professor at the University of Texas at Austin, demonstrated a remote hijacking of an unmanned aircraft by GPS guidance signals. In congressional testimony, he warned that advances in software-defined radio and the availability of GPS signal simulators may provide average hackers with the capability to interfere with unmanned aircraft operations.[27]

Humphreys recommended that non-recreational civilian unmanned aircraft weighing more than 18 pounds be required to have spoof-resistant navigation systems. More broadly, he recommended that GPS-based timing and navigation systems used in national critical infrastructure also be required to be spoof-resistant. He noted that while "[t]here is no quick, easy, and cheap fix for the civil GPS spoofing problem…reasonable, cost-effective spoofing defenses exist which, if implemented, will make successful spoofing much harder."[28] As a long-range solution, he further recommended that the Department of Homeland Security commit to funding the development and implementation of methods for performing cryptographic authentication of GPS signals, or at least for the augmented GPS signals used for civil aviation.

---

[26] Milton J. Valencia, "Ashland Man Faces Terrorism Charges," *Boston Globe*, September 29, 2011.

[27] Todd Humphreys, *Statement on the Vulnerability of Civil Unmanned Aerial Vehicles and Other Systems to Civil GPS Spoofing*, Submitted to the Subcommittee on Oversight, Investigations, and Management of the House Committee on Homeland Security, July 19, 2012.

[28] Ibid. In this context, spoofing refers to transmitting false navigation signals that could cause a drone or aircraft to veer off course.

Additionally, GAO noted that "low cost devices that jam GPS signals are prevalent."[29] However, it concluded that the issue could be mitigated by using additional navigation systems that do not rely on GPS, and/or by encrypting communications and telemetry signals.

Availability and Protection of Radiofrequency Spectrum

GAO also noted that the lack of dedicated radiofrequency spectrum for UAS operations raises the risk of lost communications links due to either unintentional or intentional signal interference.[30] Issues regarding dedicated radiofrequency spectrum for unmanned aircraft, which sometimes involve satellite control links, are typically addressed in an international forum to assure global harmonization. The appropriate forum for such determinations is International Telecommunication Union (ITU), the United Nations agency responsible for global information and communications technologies.

In December 2009, ITU issued guidance on spectrum requirements for safe operation of unmanned aircraft in non-segregated or integrated airspace. It concluded that unmanned aircraft operations will require radiofrequency spectrum for air traffic control, vehicle command and control, and sense and avoid capabilities.[31] In November 2011, it published specific guidance on the technical feasibility and advantages and disadvantages of several candidate frequency bands for beyond line of sight communications, command, and control for unmanned aircraft systems.[32] It did not formally consider or propose regulatory methods for how these frequency bands might be allocated, which would be left up to individual regulatory authorities such as the Federal Communications Commission (FCC) in the United States.

FCC has addressed radiofrequency licensing for UAVs on a case-by-case basis, much as FAA has done for certifying drone flight operations. With continued demand for spectrum from mobile broadband providers, securing dedicated radiofrequency spectrum for unmanned aircraft operations is likely to be an ongoing challenge. Moreover, the protection of radiofrequency signals to prevent potential hacking and spoofing through encryption and other methods has not yet been adequately addressed and remains a threat to the security of unmanned aircraft systems operations.

---

[29] U.S. Government Accountability Office, *Unmanned Aircraft Systems: Use in the National Airspace System and the Role of the Department of Homeland Security*, Statement of Gerald L. Dillingham, Ph.D., Director, Physical Infrastructure Issues, Before the Subcommittee on Oversight, Investigations, and Management, Committee on Homeland Security, House of Representatives, July 19, 2012, GAO-12-889T.

[30] Ibid.

[31] International Telecommunication Union, ITU-R Radiocommunication Sector of ITU, Characteristics of Unmanned Aircraft Systems and Spectrum Requirements to Support Their Safe Operation in Non-Segregated Airspace, Report ITU-R M. 2171, December, 2009, Geneva, Switzerland.

[32] International Telecommunication Union, ITU-R Radiocommunication Sector of ITU, Frequency Sharing Between Unmanned Aircraft Systems for Beyond Line of Sight Control and Non-Payload Communications Links and Other Existing and Planned Services in the Frequency Bands 13.25-13.40 GHz, 15.4-15.7 GHz, 22.5-22.55 GHz and 23.55-23.60 GHz, Report ITU-R M. 2230, November, 2011, Geneva, Switzerland.

Responsibility for Security Issues

Under the Aviation and Transportation Security Act (ATSA, P.L. 107-71), responsibility for aviation security was transferred from FAA to the newly formed Transportation Security Administration (TSA) in 2001. TSA has not specifically addressed the potential security concerns arising from the operation of drones in domestic airspace.

With regard to matters involving hacking and signal jamming, responsibility for the regulation and oversight of system security is far more complex. While TSA maintains responsibility for airspace security, FAA has regulatory authority over the certification of air vehicles. FAA has not issued certification standards for unmanned aircraft and systems, but future FAA standards may include hardware and software security and reliability assurance requirements.

FAA has worked closely with RTCA and the European Organization for Civil Aviation Equipment (EUROCAE) to define software or information assurance criteria for aircraft systems, and RTCA has released specific guidance on software considerations for airborne systems and equipment. FAA has issued advisory information for aircraft and aircraft equipment manufacturers regarding systems security and software assurance. This information indicates that the RTCA document is only one guideline manufacturers may utilize in applying systems engineering principles to ensure that aircraft component hardware and software are reliable and robust against hacking, signal interference, and other threats.[33]

Additionally, the National Information Assurance Partnership (NIAP), a partnership between the National Security Agency (NSA) and the National Institute of Standards and Technology (NIST), has established common criteria for information technology systems evaluation. Systems meeting the highest levels in the testing process are regarded as having "high robustness," meaning that they have stringent failure protections and rigorous security measures. Some avionics systems for airliners are now being tested using these common criteria methods, although such testing is not currently required. As the issue of unmanned aircraft systems certification is addressed, specific requirements for hardware and software security could be put in place. Additionally or alternatively, drone manufacturers may voluntarily apply various systems engineering and information assurance methods, such as those specified in the RTCA guidance or in the NIAP common criteria methodology, to protect systems against various information security threats.

As with many aspects of unmanned systems, a "one size fits all" approach may not be suitable, and FAA and TSA may choose to adopt a risk-based approach in addressing security matters related to unmanned aircraft operations. Under a risk-based approach, larger, more complex unmanned aircraft may be required to adopt more specific systems security and software and information assurance requirements, while more basic operational security procedures may suffice for small UAVs weighing less than 55 pounds, for example.

In general, a comprehensive approach to security issues pertaining to unmanned aircraft systems operations will likely require close coordination between TSA, FAA, FCC, manufacturers, and operators to address security issues pertaining to systems hardware and software, radiofrequency communications, and flight operations.

---

[33] Federal Aviation Administration, Advisory Circular 20-115B—Radio Technical Commission for Aeronautics, Inc. Document RTCA/DO-178B, January 11, 1993.

Airspace Restrictions

Besides safety and security, the potential impact of drone operations on airspace accessibility for other aircraft has been raised as a specific concern, particularly among operators of smaller general aviation aircraft.

One significant difference between military unmanned aircraft and unmanned aircraft operated by other public agencies or by civilian users is that the military, for many years, has negotiated with FAA to set aside airspace designated for military training, testing, and other purposes. Military airspace consists of military operations areas, military training routes, test ranges, and other restricted or prohibited airspace. Military operations areas and training routes are typically located in remote areas. While not set aside exclusively for military use, these areas and routes are charted and documented, allowing other airspace users, especially smaller general aviation aircraft, to be alert for military flight operations, including operations involving unmanned aircraft. The military has also worked with FAA to set aside specific restricted and prohibited airspace (e.g., above test sites and bombing ranges) to accommodate operations that pose greater risks to other air traffic. This airspace is charted and documented to allow pilots to avoid these areas when restrictions designating them as off limits to non-military users are in effect.

Airspace restrictions can serve as an effective tool for mitigating risks to civilian air traffic. However, their use concerns some airspace users because they pose inconveniences and sometimes raise additional safety issues. With additional restrictions, civilian pilots may be forced to fly more circuitous routes, leaving pilots with fewer options to avoid bad weather or plan for fuel stops. The Aircraft Owners and Pilots Association (AOPA), which represents more than 400,000 general aviation pilots and aviation enthusiasts across the United States, has been particularly critical of the use of restricted airspace designations to separate unmanned aircraft operations from other air traffic. AOPA has asserted that unmanned aircraft operations should not have a negative impact on general aviation operations and should not require special airspace designations, such as restricted airspace, for their operation.[34] It, however, generally supports the integration of unmanned aircraft so long as they do no harm to current manned operations.[35]

AOPA has been particularly critical of FAA's issuance of temporary flight restrictions (TFRs) to separate CBP drone operations for border surveillance from other air traffic. Testifying before the House Subcommittee on Aviation at a March 2006 hearing, AOPA Executive Vice President for Government Affairs Andrew Cebula stated that "AOPA believes that the use of 'temporary' large-scale flight restrictions for yearlong UAV operations is not appropriate and the FAA needs to fully explore the alternatives available to allow CBP (or any other agency for that matter) to secure our borders without impacting the aviation community."[36]

---

[34] Aircraft Owners and Pilots Association, *Regulatory Brief Unmanned Aircraft Systems*, Updated January 31, 2008, Frederick, MD, available at http://www.aopa.org/whatsnew/regulatory/unmanned.html.

[35] Benet J. Wilson, "Integrating Manned, Unmanned Vehicles in Airspace System," Aircraft Owners and Pilots Association, Frederick, MD, available at http://www.aopa.org/advocacy/articles/2012/120608intregating-manned-unmanned-vehicles-in-airspace-syste html.

[36] Aircraft Owners and Pilots Association, Statement of Andrew V. Cebula, Executive Vice President, Government Affairs Concerning Unmanned Aerial Vehicles in the National Airspace System, Before the Committee on Transportation and Infrastructure, Aviation Subcommittee, U.S. House of Representatives, March 29, 2006.

Industry Initiatives

The unmanned aircraft industry, collectively consisting of unmanned aircraft systems and system component manufacturers and system operators, has been cognizant of concerns regarding the operation of unmanned aircraft for civilian uses in domestic airspace. Collectively, the views of drone developers and operators worldwide are represented by the Association for Unmanned Vehicle Systems International (AUVSI). AVUSI has addressed many of the public concerns surrounding UAV operations in a voluntary industry code of conduct issued in July 2012, which is summarized in the text box below.

Voluntary Industry Code of Conduct for Drone Operations

In July 2012, the Association for Unmanned Vehicle Systems International (AUVSI) issued a voluntary industry code of conduct for the operation of unmanned aircraft systems. The code of conduct addresses concerns raised by the public and regulators regarding safety, professionalism, and respect.

With regard to safety, operators adopting the code commit to

- operating in a manner that will not present undue risk to persons or property on the surface or in the air;

- ensuring that vehicles are piloted by competent and properly trained individuals; and

- ensuring that flights are conducted only after thorough risk assessments, including consideration of weather conditions, potential failures and possible consequences, crew fitness for flight operations, airspace issues, applicable aviation regulations, frequency spectrum requirements, and the reliability, performance, and airworthiness of the aircraft.

With regard to professionalism, adopters of the code commit to

- complying with all federal, state, and local laws, ordinances, covenants, and restrictions pertaining to unmanned aircraft operations;

- operating systems as responsible members of the aviation community;

- being responsive to public needs;

- cooperating fully with federal, state, and local authorities in response to emergency deployments, mishap investigations, and media relations; and

- establishing contingency plans for all anticipated non-normal events and sharing these plans openly with all appropriate authorities.

Finally, with regard to respect, operators adopting the code commit to

- respecting the rights of other airspace users;

- respecting the privacy of individuals;

- respecting the concerns of the public regarding unmanned aircraft operations; and

- supporting improved public awareness and education regarding the operation of unmanned aircraft.

Source: Association for Unmanned Vehicle Systems International (AUVSI), Unmanned Aircraft System Operations Industry "Code of Conduct," Arlington, VA.

Eyes in the Sky: Sensor Payloads

A central issue surrounding the use of unmanned aircraft is the airborne sensors, particularly imaging sensors, that are mounted to the underbellies of these vehicles to gather data and collect images of the earth below. While these sensors may be utilized for a variety of beneficial applications, they have also raised considerable concerns regarding their potential intrusiveness, despite the aforementioned industry commitments to respect the privacy of individuals (see "Concerns over Privacy and Intrusiveness" below).

Cameras and Electro-Optical Imagers

Typical cameras and sensors placed on unmanned aircraft can collect data across a broad range of the electromagnetic spectrum, both within and beyond the range of human vision. They can provide aerial surveillance capabilities and spectral data under a wide range of lighting and atmospheric conditions. In many cases, small UAVs used in surveillance applications are simply equipped with commercial, off-the-shelf digital still photograph or video cameras. Usually, for aerial work, high-end digital cameras with image stabilization are needed to provide detailed resolution from a distance and avoid motion blur from the movement and vibration of the aircraft and the camera platform. UAVs used for detailed earth imaging are fitted with more advanced high resolution cameras. These cameras may have advanced optical features, including very large digital imaging arrays, large zoom lenses, and advanced image stabilization capabilities, allowing them to take highly detailed aerial photographs.

Captured videos and images may be transmitted for further processing or, in some cases, may be processed onboard by computer vision and video analytic software. Analytics may include tools such as scene motion detection and analysis, object detection capabilities, license plate readers, and, possibly in some cases, facial recognition software.

Drones may also be equipped with electro-optical sensors that are specifically designed for aerial operations. With regard to their imaging capabilities, electro-optical imagers are similar to high-end consumer digital cameras and typically take either still or video images within the visual electromagnetic spectrum, similar to human visual capabilities. Thus these sensors, like cameras, provide eyes in the sky when operated in good daylight and twilight visual conditions, when not obscured by clouds or fog.

Infrared Sensors

Cameras and electro-optical sensors cannot provide quality images during nighttime operations or when operating in low visibility, such as in clouds or in fog. Therefore, to augment electro-optical imaging capabilities and allow for imaging under a broader range of light conditions, sensor platforms often also include two-dimensional infrared (IR) imaging arrays. Since the longer wavelengths in the IR bands are not absorbed or attenuated by clouds or fog and are emitted by warm objects at night, IR sensors are capable of providing images beyond the capabilities or normal human sight. In the far infrared spectrum, passive millimeter wave sensors provide thermal imaging capabilities particularly for night vision and thermal imaging applications. The thermal sensing properties of IR sensors make them well suited for law enforcement and border security applications, for example, for providing eyes in the sky for foot pursuits. IR sensors are also important for command and control of UAVs operated beyond line of sight, giving operators improved situational awareness at night and in poor visibility.

Electro-optical and infrared sensors, collectively known as EO/IR sensors, are often housed together in a turret pod with gyro-stabilized gimbals that allow the sensors to move, either at the direction of a preprogrammed mission plan or from commands issued by a sensor operator remotely controlling the device (see **Figure 2**).

Figure 2. An Electro-Optical/Infrared (EO/IR) Sensor Housed in a Pod Mounted on an MQ-9 Predator B/Reaper Drone Operated by Customs and Border Protection (CBP)

Source: Customs and Border Protection (CBP).

Synthetic Aperture Radar

In addition to passive EO/IR sensors, aircraft are sometimes fitted with active synthetic aperture radar (SAR) antennas, which measure reflections of emitted microwaves to generate sensor imagery. Real time SAR imagery can penetrate through rain, fog, smoke and dust, providing surveillance capabilities in poor weather and in maritime and desert environments that can augment or replace IR and millimeter wave sensors. Some civilian applications of SAR include maritime search and rescue in adverse conditions, fire line tracking in smoke, iceberg detection and tracking, and oil spill monitoring.[37] While SAR platforms had only been available for large unmanned aircraft until recently, in 2008, defense contractors demonstrated a 2-pound SAR payload for small UAVs that was made commercially available in 2010.[38]

Specialized Sensors

Although cameras, EO/IR, and radars are the most typical types of sensors for UAV applications, unmanned aircraft can be equipped with other sensors for special applications. For example, chemical, biological, or radiological sensors may be used to collect air samples in hazardous environments. NOAA has equipped its UAVs with instruments to collect and analyze air samples.

Concerns over Privacy and Intrusiveness

While unmanned aircraft may carry a wide variety of sensor payloads for diverse applications, cameras and imaging sensors have raised particular concerns among privacy advocates who fear that widespread civilian unmanned aircraft operations could lead to abuses in monitoring, tracking, and surveilling people throughout the courses of their daily lives. Civil liberties and privacy groups including the American Civil Liberties Union (ACLU) and the Electronic Privacy Information Center (EPIC) argue that aerial drones pose a unique threat to privacy.[39] Proponents of drones have countered these arguments by underscoring the many potential benefits of domestic drone use. For example, aerial imaging of farm crops across multiple spectral bands can provide data on crop conditions and may provide critical information on the impacts of drought conditions or other factors affecting crop health. Drone proponents also contend that while unmanned aircraft have been singled out in public policy debate, the sensor technologies, imaging systems, and data collection capabilities in question are not unique to unmanned aircraft, as these devices could just as easily be installed on manned aircraft, or on utility poles, cell phone towers, and tall buildings.[40]

While the main focus of current public policy debate regarding drone use centers on the law enforcement and government use of UAVs for surveillance purposes, additional concerns have been raised regarding the commercial use of drones, including their potential use by marketing firms, private investigators, and paparazzi. While such uses may be considered intrusive by many, Fourth Amendment concerns would not specifically apply to data collections that are not conducted by or on behalf of governmental entities. Besides tracking and surveillance activities

---

[37] Mike Hanlon, "ScanEagle UAV Gets Synthetic Aperture Radar (SAR), *GizMag*, March 18, 2008, available at http://www.gizmag.com/scaneagle-uav-gets-synthetic-aperture-radar-sar/9007/.

[38] Ibid., "Insitu Announces Availability of NanoSAR—Synthetic Aperture Radar Payload." *BusinessWire*, February 23, 2010, available at http://www.businesswire.com/news/home/20100223005511/en.

[39] Jay Stanley and Catherine Crump, *Protecting Privacy From Aerial Surveillance: Recommendations for Government Use of Drones,"* American Civil Liberties Union, New York, NY, December 2011; Testimony and Statement for the Record of Amie Stepanovich, Association Litigation Counsel, Electronic Privacy Information Center, Hearing on "Using Unmanned Aerial Systems Within the Homeland: Security Game Changer?" Before the Subcommittee on Oversight, Investigations, and Management of the U.S. House of Representatives Committee on Homeland Security, July 19, 2012.

[40] For further information on the legal implications of domestic drone use, including Fourth Amendment and other privacy concerns, see CRS Report R42701, *Drones in Domestic Surveillance Operations: Fourth Amendment Implications and Legislative Responses*, by Richard M. Thompson II.

---

that raise specific privacy concerns, civilian unmanned aircraft operations may raise additional concerns regarding their potential intrusiveness. Various potential commercial uses, such as aerial advertising (using drones to tow banners or display other targeted visual advertisements), may not raise privacy concerns per se, but may nonetheless be regarded by some as intrusive and a nuisance because of aircraft noise and visual distraction.

FAA's authority over specific uses for civilian unmanned aircraft appears limited. As a matter of law, aircraft have privileged access to navigable airspace. U.S. law generally maintains that equal access and availability of navigable airspace to all users are basic principles underlying the national airspace system, so long as safety and national security are not compromised. Notably, 49 U.S.C. Section 40101(c) (2) specifies that FAA, in carrying out its authority to regulate aviation, shall consider the public right of freedom of transit through the navigable airspace.

Navigable airspace is defined in statute as that airspace above minimum flight altitudes prescribed by regulation, including airspace needed to ensure safety during takeoff and landing.[41] Away from airports, minimum altitudes defining navigable airspace are largely predicated on safety concerns and depend on characteristics of the aircraft and risks posed to persons and property on the ground. In general, navigable airspace is considered to be 500 feet above ground level and higher, except in congested areas where the minimum safe altitude rises to 1,000 feet above the highest obstacle within a 2,000-foot radius of the aircraft's position at any given time.[42] In sparsely populated areas and over water, navigable airspace can be considered to be much lower, so long as operators assure that they can make an emergency landing after an engine failure without undue hazard to persons or property on the ground. Moreover, helicopters, powered parachutes, and powered hang gliders can be operated below established minimums so long as operations are conducted without hazard to persons or property on the ground, and so long as helicopters follow certain prescribed routes and altitudes when defined, usually for noise abatement purposes. Minimum altitudes for drones are yet to be defined. However, unregulated model aircraft are generally permitted below 400 feet, outside of navigable airspace for most manned aircraft.

Small low-flying drones may pose particular concerns regarding intrusiveness, especially if they become widely proliferated in urban and suburban areas. For example, it is imaginable that drones displaying advertising material might hover noisily above a beach, or that a magazine might deploy a drone equipped with high-resolution cameras to photograph a celebrity's garden party. As FAA is primarily concerned with balancing safety concerns with its obligation to facilitate access to navigable airspace, it is likely to tread lightly with regard to matters pertaining to the regulation of specific drone uses based upon their perceived intrusiveness.

Although FAA may be reluctant to address such issues, matters pertaining to the use of domestic airspace generally fall exclusively within its purview. 49 U.S.C. §40103(a)(1) specifies that the federal government has exclusive sovereignty of domestic airspace, thus significantly limiting state and local governments from promulgating laws, regulations, or ordinances affecting access to the national airspace system. This may make it particularly difficult for state and local governments to restrict or regulate the use of drones, including imposing limitations on noise.

---

[41] 49 U.S.C. §40102(a)(32).

[42] See 14 C.F.R. §91.119 Minimum safe altitudes: General.

On the federal level, landowner rights with regard to the navigable airspace above private property are similarly restricted. The Supreme Court has stated that "the air is a public highway, as Congress has declared. Were that not true, every transcontinental flight would subject the operator to countless trespass suits. Common sense revolts at the idea."[43]

While the concept of the air as a public highway has largely overturned the ancient Roman concept that the owner of a land also holds title to the air above, it does not preclude civilians from potentially seeking civil remedies in the courts against aircraft operators flying overhead or in close proximity to an individual's land. This may potentially include civil action against private or commercial drone operators, if damage or interference can be demonstrated. It may also include claims against federal drone operators if the operations are considered to constitute a taking of property by the government because the aviation activity results in a loss of use or a loss of enjoyment of the property. The Fifth Amendment, among other things, protects citizens from a taking of private property for public use without just compensation.

In these matters, case law relating to aircraft noise may have particular relevance to potential landowner actions in response to nuisances and interference caused by drone operations. Nuisance suits pertaining to aviation noise have allowed recovery for annoyance, inconvenience, discomfort, and mental and emotional distress, as well as for property damage. Additionally, citizens have been successful in actions against the federal government under the "just compensation" clause of the Fifth Amendment in cases where federal aviation operations, usually from military airbases or military training areas, have interfered with the use and enjoyment of private land, thereby constituting a "taking" of the land without any formal exercise of powers of eminent domain. To the extent that case law regarding aircraft noise from the early days of civil jet air transportation may bolster potential legal challenges to drone operations, history suggests that the introduction of civilian drones in the national airspace system is likely to be a highly contentious matter.

Author Contact Information

Bart Elias
Specialist in Aviation Policy
belias@crs.loc.gov, 7-7771

---

[43] United States v. Causby, 328 U.S. 256, 260-61 (1946).